how to draw
cartoons

igloo

how to draw cartoons

You don't need lots of expensive equipment to start cartooning. Here's a list of the basic materials.

Paper, and lots of it. Plain photocopy or laser printer paper is inexpensive and has a smooth surface, so it's easy to erase your mistakes. Scrap paper is useful when you're experimenting, and a small sketch pad comes in handy if you see something interesting when you're out and about.

Pencils – soft and hard. Softer pencils are good for sketching and shading, and are easy to erase. Harder pencils have a sharper point, so you can use them for the finer details. You'll need a good eraser and a pencil sharpener, too.

A small ruler is useful and you might want to buy a stencil for drawing circles and ovals. (Otherwise you can draw around something like a cup or bottle cap for a perfect circle.)

You will need a waterproof black pen to ink over your pencil drawings. These come in varying thicknesses, so you could get a selection.

Finally, for coloring your finished artwork, you will need some colored pencils, felt pens, or paints and paintbrushes.

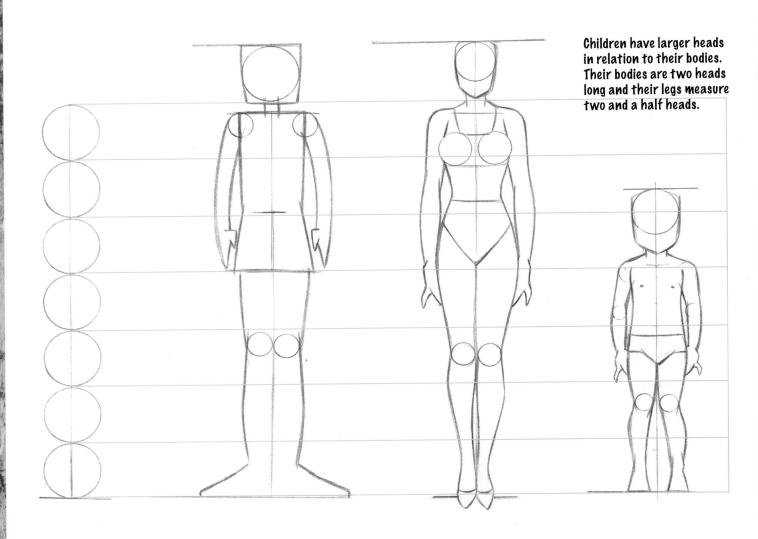

Children have larger heads in relation to their bodies. Their bodies are two heads long and their legs measure two and a half heads.

If you measure a person's head from the crown to the chin, you can work out the proportions of the body. The adult torso is the equivalent of three heads and the legs are four heads long.

Human proportions

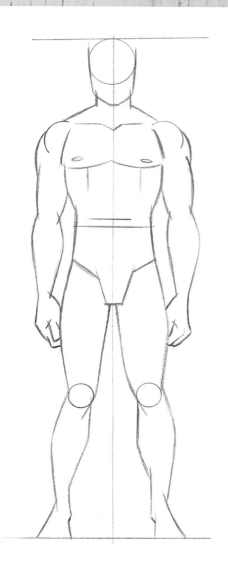

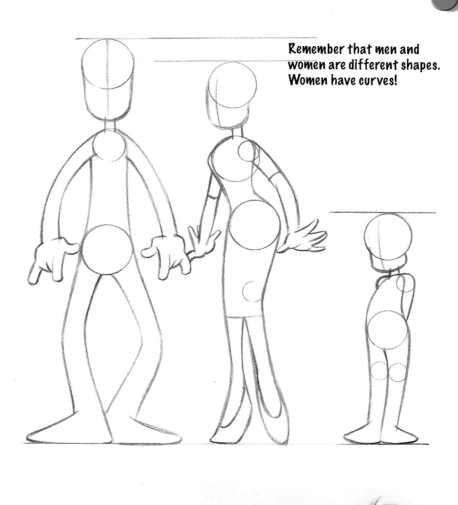

Remember that men and women are different shapes. Women have curves!

... and teenagers are a species of their own!

how to draw **cartoons**

Once you've mastered the basics, it's time to
bring your figures to life. Try making simple
sketches of people in different positions to
build up a library of useful material.

It's a good idea to carry
a pencil and paper at all
times, so you can do a
quick sketch if you spot
someone doing something
interesting.

Body language

Sometimes it's easier to use a photograph for reference than trying to capture someone moving in real life.

When figures are running fast they have both feet off the ground. As the right leg goes forward the right arm moves backward and vice versa.

On the move

Adding a shadow beneath a figure's foot shows that it is off the ground.

how to draw **cartoons**

Now try drawing the more realistic animals on these pages, following the simple step-by-step guides.

How to draw animals

how to draw **cartoons**

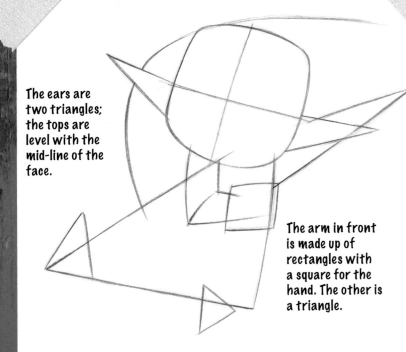

The ears are two triangles; the tops are level with the mid-line of the face.

The arm in front is made up of rectangles with a square for the hand. The other is a triangle.

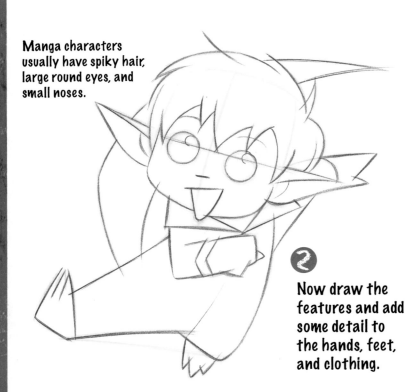

Manga characters usually have spiky hair, large round eyes, and small noses.

2 Now draw the features and add some detail to the hands, feet, and clothing.

This character's head is square with rounded corners. Draw a cross through the middle, so you can position the features. The body and feet are triangles and the tail arches from the middle of the body over the top of the head.

Experiment with different mouth shapes. Manga characters normally have small mouths unless they are laughing, then the mouth takes over most of the face, exaggerating the emotion.

MANGA STYLE

❸

Complete your drawing, rounding off the hands and feet and adding more detail to the ears, hair, tail, and clothing.

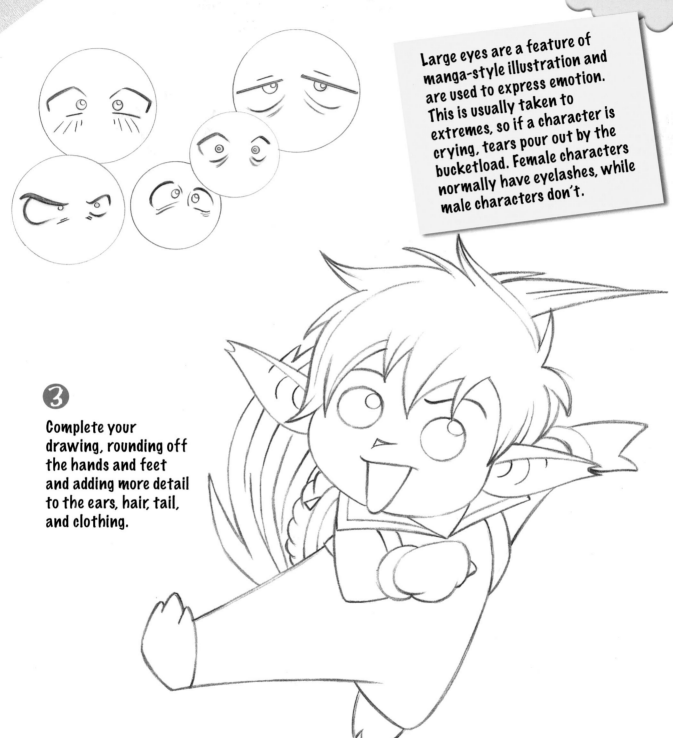

4

When you are happy with your drawing, ink over the lines using a black pen, then erase the pencil marks.

⑤

Now color your character. Use a lighter tone for the highlights and darker shades for the shadows.

Manga characters often have brightly-colored hair.

Add a shadow on the ground beneath the figure.

how to draw **cartoons**

1

Draw a large oval shape to form the body of the vehicle, then position the wheels, headlamps, mirrors, and fins.

Only three of the four wheels are visible.

2

Fill in the details, such as the interior, make the fins a more rounded shape, and square off the back.

3

Now it's time to add the finishing touches.

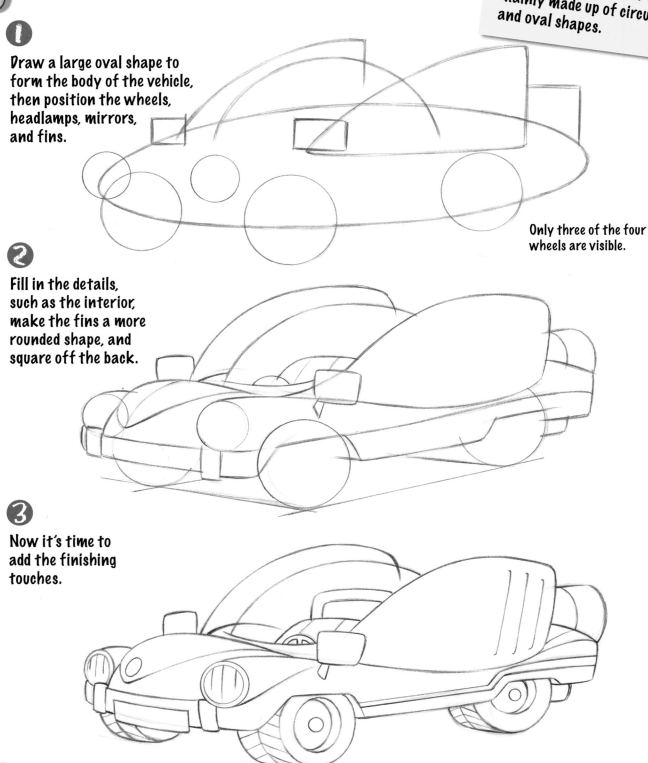

4

When you are happy with your drawing, ink over the lines using a black pen, then erase the pencil marks.

5

Now color your drawing. This vehicle has been flat-colored, without any shading.

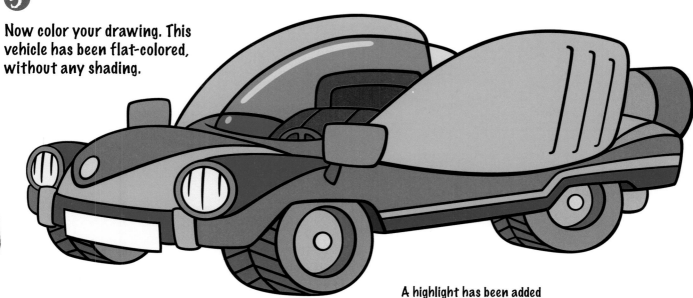

A highlight has been added to the windshield to show that it is made of glass.

how to draw cartoons

1 A typical superhero has a prominent chest with a narrow waist and hips. Men always have a very defined jawline – square and manly.

A superhero's cape flies in the breeze (even when he's standing still), but he never has a hair out of place.

3 A jutting jaw, with a cleft in the chin, and furrowed brows will give your character the classic superhero expression.

2 Male characters have more muscles than the average guy, but beware of making your superhero look like a balloon man.

4 When you are happy with your drawing, ink over the lines using a black pen, then erase the pencil marks.

5 Now color your drawing. This character has been flat-colored, without any shading.

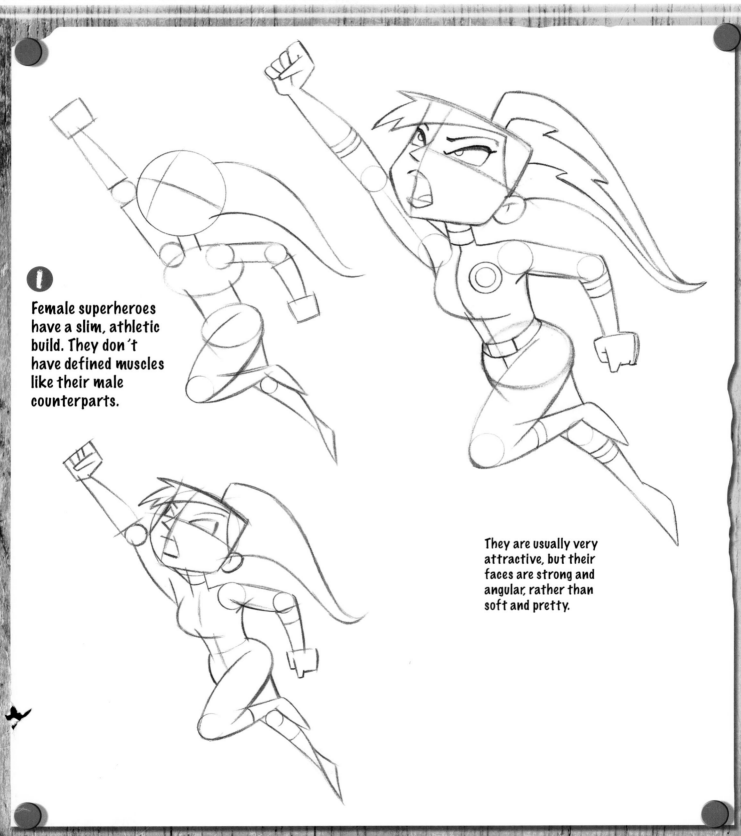

1 Female superheroes have a slim, athletic build. They don't have defined muscles like their male counterparts.

They are usually very attractive, but their faces are strong and angular, rather than soft and pretty.

2

When your pencil drawing is complete, go over the lines with a black pen and erase all the pencil marks.

3

Now color your drawing. This illustration has been flat-colored, without any shading.

how to draw cartoons

① First draw the basic outline of your character.

② Sketch in horizontal and vertical lines to mark the center of the face and of the body.

③ Now add the details to the features, hands, and clothing.

Unlike the hands of most of the classic cartoon animals, human characters' hands have four fingers and one thumb.

The faces of classic cartoon characters follow all the normal rules – the eyes are one eye width apart and are positioned halfway down the head, the nose and ears are just below the midline of the face, and the mouth is halfway between the nose and the chin.

4

Complete your illustration by drawing the fishing line, and the gnome's glasses and belt buckle.

When your pencil drawing
is finished, go over the lines
with a black pen and erase
all the pencil marks.

6

Now color your drawing. This illustration has quite complex shading and highlights.

how to draw cartoons

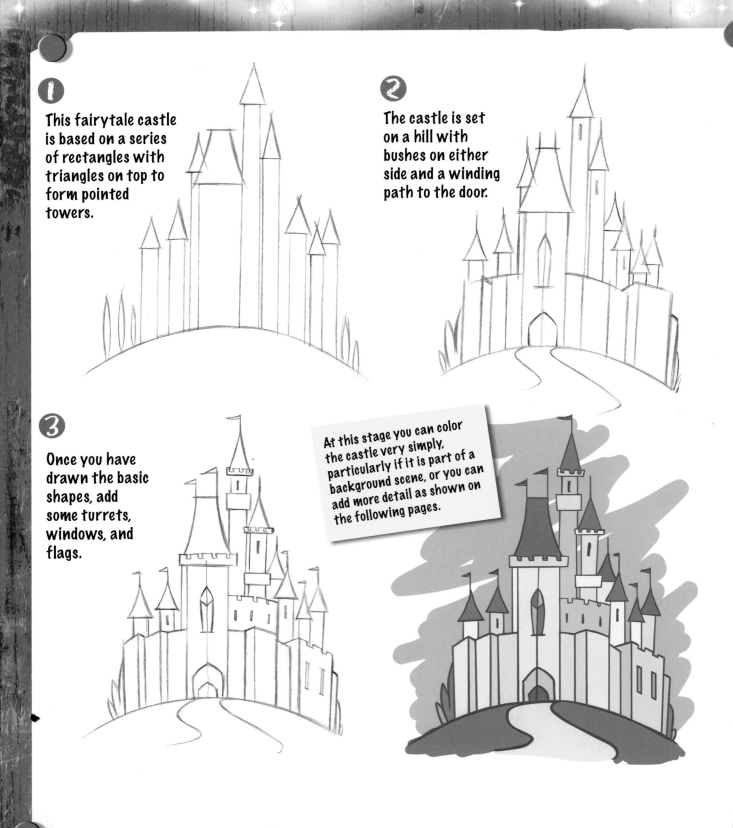

1 This fairytale castle is based on a series of rectangles with triangles on top to form pointed towers.

2 The castle is set on a hill with bushes on either side and a winding path to the door.

3 Once you have drawn the basic shapes, add some turrets, windows, and flags.

At this stage you can color the castle very simply, particularly if it is part of a background scene, or you can add more detail as shown on the following pages.

4

If you want to make more of a feature of your castle, continue adding details, such as bricks and roof tiles. It's not necessary to draw each brick or tile. Just a few will do.

A few stones, tufts of grass and extra bushes will make the landscape more interesting.

5

Adding shading will give depth to your drawing.

6

The linework for this castle has been done in "local color" (a darker shade of the background color) rather than black. This gives a more subtle effect, and adds distance if black linework is used for an object or character in the foreground of the illustration.

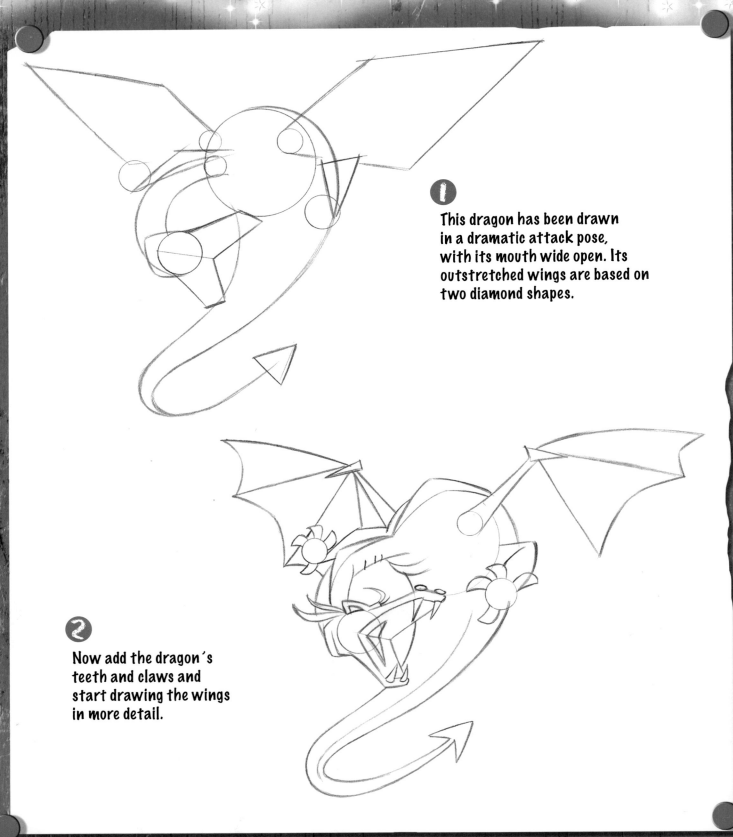

1

This dragon has been drawn in a dramatic attack pose, with its mouth wide open. Its outstretched wings are based on two diamond shapes.

2

Now add the dragon's teeth and claws and start drawing the wings in more detail.

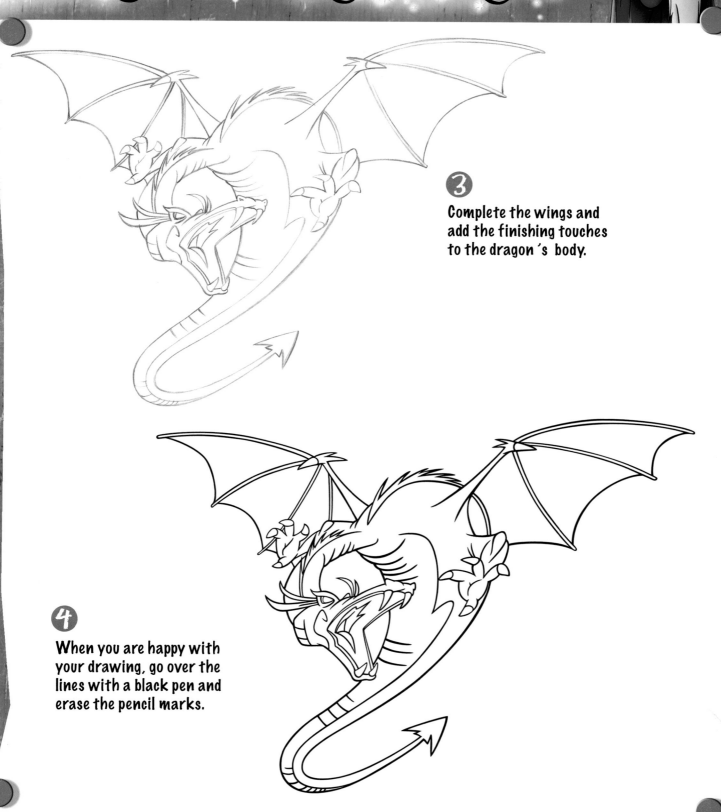

3

Complete the wings and add the finishing touches to the dragon's body.

4

When you are happy with your drawing, go over the lines with a black pen and erase the pencil marks.

5

Now color your drawing. Here
the use of shading and highlights
really brings the dragon to life.
It looks as if it's about to leap
out from the page.